RANJOT SINGH CHAHAL

How to Speak Business English with Confidence

A Guide to Boosting Business English Proficiency

Rana Books

First published by Rana Books Uk 2023

Copyright © 2023 by Ranjot Singh Chahal

First edition

Contents

Acknowledgement

I extend my heartfelt gratitude to all those who contributed to the creation of this book. First and foremost, I would like to express my appreciation to my family for their unwavering support and encouragement throughout this journey.

A special thanks goes to my mentors and educators who have shaped my understanding of business English and communication skills. Your guidance has been invaluable.

I am also indebted to the team at Rana Books UK for their dedication in bringing this book to life.

To my friends and colleagues who provided valuable insights and feedback, thank you for your input.

Lastly, I want to acknowledge the readers whose interest and enthusiasm continually inspire me to delve deeper into the realm of business English communication.

Thank you all for being a part of this endeavor.

Ranjot Singh Chahal

About Author

Ranjot Chahal, also known as Jot Chahal, is a gifted author and poet originating from the Mansa district of Punjab. Currently residing in Cardiff, Wales, United Kingdom, he recently completed his master's degree at Cardiff Metropolitan University in June 2023. Ranjot has garnered significant recognition for his contemplative literary works, which encompass an array of poetry and quotes reflecting his distinctive outlook on life.

Born into a Sikh family, Ranjot has always held a profound respect for his community's rich cultural and spiritual heritage. His literary creations serve as a testament to his profound affection and enthusiasm for literature, effectively bridging the gap between classical and contemporary literary realms.

Ranjot's literary works extend across languages, with publications available in Punjabi, English, and Hindi, thus rendering his artistry accessible to a broad spectrum of readers. His compositions seamlessly intertwine spirituality, philosophy, and personal encounters, drawing admiration for their profoundness and originality.

Notably, Ranjot Chahal has ventured into the realm of audio books, expanding his literary influence through auditory channels. His dedication and ardor for his craft have propelled him into the literary spotlight, earning the admiration of readers worldwide. With his recent academic achievement—a master's degree from Cardiff Metropolitan University in June 2023—he continues to fortify his position as an emerging luminary within the literary world. Ranjot's endeavors are set to persistently inspire and enlighten readers, solidifying his imprint on the landscape of literature.

I

Fundamentals of Business English

"Fundamentals of Business English" forms the cornerstone of effective corporate communication. From mastering sentence structure to acquiring essential business vocabulary, this section lays the groundwork for confident interactions. Explore the intricate nuances of grammar, word usage, and terminology, equipping yourself with the tools needed to excel in the business world.

Introduction

The Importance of Business English : Business English is not just another language skill; it plays a crucial role in today's global business landscape. With English being the lingua franca of international business communication having proficiency in Business English can significantly enhance professional opportunities and success.

Here are some reasons why Business English is important:

1. Global Communication: English has become the common language for business communication worldwide. Whether it's negotiations meetings or presentations proficiency in Business English enables effective communication with clients partners and colleagues from diverse backgrounds. It fosters better understanding collaboration and business relationships across borders.

2. Professional Networking: Business English proficiency enhances networking opportunities. It helps professionals build connections attend conferences participate in industry events and engage with colleagues and key stakeholders. Effective Business English skills enable individuals to articulate their ideas express themselves succinctly and establish credibility which are vital for networking success.

3. Career Advancement: In an increasingly competitive job market Business English proficiency sets candidates apart. Employers seek individuals who can confidently communicate and interact with international clients global teams

and multinational companies. Strong Business English skills demonstrate adaptability professionalism and a commitment to professional growth making individuals more attractive to employers and opening doors to better career opportunities.

4. Cross-Cultural Understanding: Business English provides a platform for cultural understanding and sensitivity. When communicating with people from different backgrounds understanding cultural nuances and adapting communication styles appropriately is crucial. A solid grasp of Business English helps individuals navigate these cultural complexities avoiding misunderstandings and fostering respect and collaboration.

5. Effective Business Writing: Clear and concise written communication is vital in the business world. Proficiency in Business English enables professionals to craft professional emails reports proposals and other business documents with precision clarity and persuasiveness. Well-written communications not only convey professionalism but also enhance credibility and contribute to successful business outcomes.

6. International Business Opportunities: English-speaking countries such as the United States the United Kingdom Canada and Australia hold significant economic opportunities for businesses. Proficiency in Business English opens doors for international trade investment and partnerships. It facilitates market expansion enables access to global talent and empowers professionals to explore international business opportunities.

7. Personal Development: Developing Business English skills boosts personal growth and confidence. It provides individuals with a sense of self-assurance and empowers them to express their thoughts and ideas more effectively. Strong Business English skills enable individuals to participate actively in meetings negotiate agreements present ideas and contribute meaningfully to business discussions ultimately leading to personal and professional growth .

The role of communication in business success : Communication plays a crucial role in the success of any business. It is the foundation upon which relationships are built ideas are exchanged and decisions are made. Strong communication skills and effective communication strategies can greatly enhance a company's overall performance and competitiveness. Here are some key aspects where communication has a significant impact on business success:

1. Internal Communication: Effective internal communication is vital for the smooth functioning of an organization. It ensures that employees have a clear understanding of organizational goals expectations and their roles. Open and transparent communication fosters a positive work environment boosts employee morale and promotes collaboration and teamwork.

2. External Communication: Successful businesses must communicate effectively with external stakeholders such as customers clients suppliers investors and the general public. Clear and concise communication helps build trust credibility and strong relationships with these stakeholders. It allows businesses to deliver their value proposition effectively understand customer needs and respond to market trends and demands.

3. Decision Making: Communication enables effective decision making within a business. Collaboration and the exchange of information ideas and perspectives lead to more informed and well-rounded decisions. When employees are encouraged to share their thoughts and opinions it promotes innovation and creative problem-solving.

4. Conflict Resolution: In every business conflicts and disagreements are inevitable. Effective communication skills are essential in resolving conflicts in a professional and constructive manner. Clear communication helps identify the root causes of conflicts facilitates productive conversations and allows parties to reach mutually acceptable resolutions. This not only promotes a harmonious work environment but also strengthens relationships

among employees.

5. Customer Service: Communication is the backbone of exceptional customer service. Timely and effective communication with customers helps to understand their needs address their concerns and exceed their expectations. Businesses that prioritize communication with customers build trust loyalty and a positive brand image.

6. Business Relationships: Strong communication skills are crucial for building and maintaining partnerships and business relationships. Effective communication helps establish rapport understanding and mutual respect with clients suppliers and other stakeholders. It strengthens relationships and opens doors to new opportunities collaborations and business growth.

7. Crisis Management: During times of crisis or unforeseen events clear and timely communication is of utmost importance. Businesses need to communicate transparently and honestly with employees customers and stakeholders to manage the situation effectively. Open communication helps mitigate damage maintain trust and protect the reputation of the business.

In summary effective communication is the backbone of business success. It facilitates internal cohesion strengthens relationships with external stakeholders supports decision making resolves conflicts enhances customer service builds business relationships and aids in crisis management. Investing in communication skills and developing effective communication strategies can significantly contribute to the overall success and sustainability of a business.

The role of communication in business success : Having strong English proficiency in the business world can provide several significant advantages. Here are some of them:

1. Global Communication: English is the most widely spoken language for

business communication worldwide. By having strong English proficiency you can effectively communicate with clients colleagues and partners from different countries and cultures. This ability to connect with a global audience enhances your chances of building strong professional relationships and expanding your business network.

2. Access to Market Opportunities: English proficiency opens the door to access a larger market. Many multinational companies conduct business in English and proficiency in the language gives you a competitive edge in international trade. It allows you to expand your customer base enter new markets and explore new business opportunities across borders.

3. Enhancing Professional Credibility: A strong command of English helps boost your professional credibility. It demonstrates your competence and reliability to clients and business partners showcasing your ability to engage in negotiations present ideas and build trust. This credibility can lead to increased business partnerships collaborations and career advancements.

4. Improved Job Prospects: In many industries English proficiency is a highly sought-after skill by employers. Companies with a global presence often require employees who can effectively communicate in English to engage in international transactions and collaborations. Having a strong command of English on your resume can broaden your job prospects increase your employability and potentially lead to higher-paying positions.

5. Access to Resources and Knowledge: English is the dominant language for business literature research papers and industry publications. By being proficient in English you can access a vast amount of information stay updated with the latest industry trends and expand your knowledge base. This access to resources can make you more informed and capable of making better business decisions.

6. Effective Communication within Multicultural Teams: In today's globalized

business environment many organizations work with multicultural teams consisting of professionals from diverse linguistic and cultural backgrounds. English serves as a common language for these teams to communicate and collaborate effectively. By mastering English you can bridge communication barriers facilitate teamwork and contribute to a harmonious and productive work environment.

7. Enhanced Presentation and Negotiation Skills: English proficiency can greatly improve your ability to deliver persuasive presentations engage in successful negotiations and articulate your ideas precisely. This skill is particularly important when pitching ideas participating in conferences or closing business deals. Effective communication in English allows you to convey your message clearly persuasively and confidently increasing your chances of achieving positive outcomes.

In conclusion strong English proficiency in the business world provides numerous advantages by facilitating global communication expanding market opportunities enhancing professional credibility improving job prospects giving access to resources and knowledge facilitating effective communication within multicultural teams and boosting presentation and negotiation skills. Investing in developing English language skills can significantly benefit your business and career prospects in today's interconnected world.

Basic Grammar and Vocabulary

Grammar refers to the structural rules and principles governing the composition of sentences while vocabulary refers to the words that constitute a language. Understanding grammar and having a good vocabulary are essential for effective communication.

1. Parts of Speech:
   - Noun: A word that represents a person place thing or idea. Examples: dog city love.
   - Verb: A word that expresses an action state or occurrence. Examples: run eat sleep.
   - Adjective: A word that describes or modifies a noun. Examples: big happy red.
   - Adverb: A word that describes or modifies a verb adjective or another adverb. Examples: quickly very well.
   - Pronoun: A word used instead of a noun to avoid repetition. Examples: he she they.
   - Preposition: A word that shows the relationship of a noun or pronoun to another word. Examples: in on at.
   - Conjunction: A word that connects words phrases or clauses. Examples: and but or.
   - Interjection: A word or short phrase that expresses strong emotion. Examples: wow oh ouch.

2. Sentence Structure:

- Subject and Predicate: Every sentence has a subject (the one that performs the action) and a predicate (the action being performed). Example: John (subject) runs (predicate).

- Noun Phrase: A group of words that functions as a noun in a sentence. Example: The big black cat sat on the mat.

- Verb Phrase: A group of words that functions as a verb in a sentence. Example: She was baking a delicious cake.

- Clause: A group of words that contains a subject and a verb. Clauses can be independent (can stand alone as a sentence) or dependent (cannot stand alone). Example: I love reading (independent clause although it takes up a lot of my time (dependent clause).

- Sentence Types: Sentences can be declarative (states a fact or opinion interrogative (asks a question imperative (gives a command or exclamatory (expresses strong emotion). Example: Declarative - It is a beautiful day. Interrogative - How are you? Imperative - Please close the door. Exclamatory - What a stunning view!

3. Vocabulary:
- Synonyms: Words that have similar or identical meanings. Examples: happy and joyful big and large.

- Antonyms: Words that have opposite meanings. Examples: happy and sad hot and cold.

- Homophones: Words that sound the same but have different meanings or spellings. Examples: there their they're.

- Idioms: Phrases that have a different meaning from the literal interpretation. Examples: kick the bucket (meaning to die a piece of cake (meaning something easy).

- Collocations: Words that frequently occur together. Examples: fast food heavy rain make a decision.

Remember effective communication involves using proper grammar and employing a wide range of vocabulary. Regular practice and exposure to different types of sentences and words will help improve your language skills.

Sentence structure and word order : English sentence structure and word order typically follow a subject-verb-object (SVO) pattern. This means that the subject comes first followed by the verb and then the object. However there are variations and exceptions to this structure depending on different sentence types and functions.

1. Basic SVO Structure:
   - Example: She (subject) loves (verb) chocolate (object).

2. Questions:
   - In interrogative sentences the word order is often inverted with the verb preceding the subject.
   Example: Are (verb) you (subject) coming to the party?

3. Negation:
   - When using negative constructions the word "not" is typically placed after the auxiliary verb or the main verb.
   Example: They (subject) do not (negation) want (verb) to go (object).

4. Object-Subject-Verb (OSV) Structure:
   - In certain cases such as after certain adverbial expressions or in some types of clauses the object can be placed before the subject and verb.
   Example: Into the room (object) walked (verb) the cat (subject).

5. Imperative Sentences:
   - In imperative sentences the subject (you) is often left implicit and the verb comes first.
   Example: (You) Close the door.

6. Adverb Placement:
   - Adverbs generally come after the verb in the sentence although there can be flexibility in their placement depending on the intended emphasis.
   Example: He (subject) quickly (adverb) ran (verb) to catch the bus (object).

7. Indirect Objects:

- When there are both indirect and direct objects the indirect object (recipient or beneficiary) usually comes before the direct object.

Example: She (subject) gave (verb) her sister (indirect object) a present (direct object).

8. Complex Sentences:

- English allows for various sentence structures with subordinate clauses such as conditional clauses relative clauses and complement clauses. In these cases the word order can differ depending on the specific clause type and its function within the sentence.

Example: If (subordinate clause) I see (verb) him (object I will say hello (main clause).

It's important to note that while the SVO word order is common in English it is not universal across all languages and there can be additional variations and exceptions. To fully understand sentence structure and word order it's essential to study and analyze different sentence types and their specific rules.

Nouns verbs adjectives and adverbs :

Nouns:

Nouns are words that represent people places things or ideas. They can be singular or plural.

Examples:
- Person: John teacher friend
- Place: London park school
- Thing: book car chair
- Idea: love happiness freedom

Verbs:

Verbs are words that describe actions occurrences or states of being. They show what the subject of a sentence does or experiences.

Examples:
- Action: run jump eat
- Occurrence: happen arrive fall
- State of being: is exist seem

Adjectives:

Adjectives are words that describe or modify nouns or pronouns. They provide additional information about the noun.

Examples:
- Size: big small tiny
- Color: red blue green
- Shape: round square triangular
- Qualities: intelligent strong beautiful

Adverbs:

Adverbs are words that modify verbs adjectives or other adverbs. They provide more information about how when where or to what extent an action is performed.

Examples:
- How: quickly slowly well
- When: yesterday today soon
- Where: here there inside
- To what extent: very extremely quite

Here are some sentences showcasing the use of nouns verbs adjectives and adverbs together:

- The brave (adjective) firefighter (noun) quickly (adverb) extinguished (verb) the blazing (adjective) fire (noun).

- Sarah (noun) carefully (adverb) walked (verb) along the narrow (adjective) path (noun) in the dark (adjective) forest (noun).

- The delicious (adjective) chocolate (noun) cake (noun) was eagerly (adverb) devoured (verb) by the hungry (adjective) children (noun).

- The bright (adjective) sun (noun) shines (verb) brightly (adverb) in the clear (adjective) sky (noun).

These examples demonstrate how different word categories work together to create meaningful and descriptive sentences in English.

Common business-related vocabulary :

1. Revenue: The total income generated by a company from its operations.

2. Expenses: The costs incurred by a company to run its business.

3. Profit: The amount of money left after subtracting expenses from revenue.

4. Loss: The negative difference between revenue and expenses.

5. Gross profit: The profit before deducting taxes and other expenses.

6. Net profit: The profit after deducting all expenses.

7. Sales: The act of selling products or services.

8. Marketing: The activities performed to promote and sell products or services.

9. Advertising: The paid promotion of products or services to reach potential customers.

10. Customer: An individual or business that purchases goods or services from a company.

11. Client: A customer who has an ongoing relationship with a company often for services.

12. Supplier: A company or individual that provides goods or services to another company.

13. Inventory: The stock of goods a company has available for sale.

14. Assets: Items of value owned by a company such as cash equipment or

property.

15. Liabilities: Debts or financial obligations of a company.

16. Equity: The value of ownership in a company calculated as assets minus liabilities.

17. Cash flow: The movement of cash into or out of a company.

18. Budget: A financial plan that outlines expected revenue and expenses.

19. Forecast: A prediction of future sales expenses or financial outcomes.

20. Investment: Allocating money or resources with the expectation of future returns.

21. Entrepreneur: An individual who starts and operates a business.

22. Partnership: A legal structure where two or more individuals share ownership and responsibilities for a business.

23. Corporation: A legal entity separate from its owners offering limited liability for shareholders.

24. Sole proprietorship: A business owned and operated by one person.

25. Limited liability company (LLC): A business structure that combines the benefits of a corporation and partnership providing limited liability to its owners.

26. Stakeholder: Any individual or group affected by or with an interest in a company's activities.

27. Board of Directors: A group elected by the shareholders to oversee and make important decisions for a company.

28. CEO (Chief Executive Officer): The highest-ranking executive responsible for overall management of a company.

29. CFO (Chief Financial Officer): The executive responsible for managing a company's financial activities.

30. HR (Human Resources): The department responsible for managing employee recruitment training and welfare.

31. Procurement: The process of obtaining goods or services for a company at the best possible value.

32. Outsourcing: Contracting work or services to an external provider rather than handling them in-house.

33. Supply chain: The network of individuals organizations and activities

involved in the production and distribution of goods or services.

34. Logistics: The management of the flow of goods or services from the point of origin to the point of consumption.

35. Quality control: The processes and activities implemented to ensure that products or services meet the desired standards.

36. Leadership: The ability to guide and influence others toward achieving a common goal.

37. Teamwork: Collaborative efforts of a group of individuals to achieve a common objective.

38. Organizational culture: The values beliefs and behaviors that shape the unique environment of a company.

39. Mission statement: A brief statement that defines a company's purpose and goals.

40. Vision statement: A declaration of a company's aspirations and desired future state.

41. Innovation: The introduction of new ideas products or practices to improve efficiency or create value.

42. Entrepreneurship: The process of identifying and pursuing opportunities to start a new business or venture.

43. Market research: The gathering and analysis of data about customers competitors and market trends to make informed business decisions.

44. Business plan: A written document that outlines a company's goals strategies and financial projections.

45. SWOT analysis: An evaluation of a company's strengths weaknesses opportunities and threats to make strategic decisions.

46. ROI (Return on Investment): A measure of the profitability of an investment typically calculated as a percentage.

47. Break-even point: The level of sales at which total revenue equals total expenses resulting in neither profit nor loss.

48. KPI (Key Performance Indicator): A measurable value that indicates how well a company is achieving its objectives.

49. Market share: The proportion of total market sales that a company captures.

50. Competitive advantage: A characteristic or factor that allows a company to outperform its competitors.

51. Mergers and acquisitions: The consolidation of two or more companies through various means such as buyouts or takeovers.

52. IPO (Initial Public Offering): The first sale of a company's stock to the public.

53. Dividend: A portion of a company's profits distributed to shareholders.

54. Return on Equity (ROE): A financial indicator that measures the return generated on shareholder's equity.

55. Risk management: The process of identifying analyzing and mitigating potential risks that could impact a company's objectives.

56. Competitive analysis: Evaluating the strengths and weaknesses of competitors to develop strategies for outperforming them.

57. Stakeholder analysis: Identifying the interests concerns and influence of various stakeholders to effectively manage relationships.

58. Market segmentation: Dividing a target market into distinct groups based on characteristics behaviors or needs.

59. Product development: The process of creating and enhancing products or services to meet customer needs.

60. Project management: Planning organizing and controlling resources and activities to achieve specific project goals.

61. Contract: A legally binding agreement between two or more parties outlining the terms and conditions of their relationship.

62. Confidentiality: The protection of sensitive information from unauthorized access or disclosure.

63. Ethics: Moral principles and values that guide behavior in business and other contexts.

64. Compliance: Adherence to laws regulations and industry standards.

65. Intellectual property: Legal rights protecting creations of the mind such as inventions trademarks or artistic works.

66. Inflation: The general increase in prices over time reducing the purchasing power of money.

67. Recession: A significant decline in economic activity often characterized

by decreased production employment and spending.

68. Globalization: The increasing interconnectedness and integration of economies cultures and societies worldwide.

69. Trade: The exchange of goods or services between individuals organizations or countries.

70. Outsourcing: Contracting work or services to an external provider rather than handling in.

Accounting process recording analyzing and financial a. The verification records by auditor.ive reward offered behavior performance. Financial a investment.

Tar: tax duty imported.

and demand: The interaction between the availability and desire for a product or service determining its price.

77. Market research: The gathering and analysis of data about customers competitors and market trends to make informed business decisions.

Business Writing Skills

Business writing skills are essential for effective communication in a professional setting. They enable individuals to convey information clearly concisely and professionally. Here are some key aspects of business writing skills with examples:

1. Clarity and Conciseness:
   - Clear and concise writing ensures that the message is easily understood. For example:
   Unclear: "We're thinking about implementing a new strategy that might work well but we need to discuss it further."
   Clear: "We propose implementing a new strategy. Let's discuss it in our next meeting."

2. Professional Tone:
   - Using a professional tone creates a professional image and establishes credibility. For example:
   Unprofessional: "Hey what's up? I need those reports ASAP."
   Professional: "Hello could you please prioritize the delivery of the reports as soon as possible?"

3. Audience Understanding:
   - Writing with the audience in mind helps tailor the message to their needs. For example:
   General: "Our latest product is great for everyone."

Targeted: "Our latest product addresses the needs of busy professionals offering time-saving features."

4. Structure and Organization:
- Organized writing with a clear structure makes it easier for readers to follow. For example:
Unorganized: "Here are some thoughts on the new marketing campaign: budget target audience ROI."
Organized: "Regarding the new marketing campaign I would like to discuss the budget target audience and expected return on investment (ROI)."

5. Grammar and Punctuation:
- Proper grammar and punctuation contribute to clarity and professionalism. For example:
Incorrect: "Their going to present they're results tomorrow."
Correct: "They're going to present their results tomorrow."

6. Use of Active Voice:
- Active voice makes writing more direct and engaging. For example:
Passive: "The error was fixed by the IT department."
Active: "The IT department fixed the error."

7. Persuasive Writing:
- Persuasive writing techniques can influence readers and achieve desired outcomes. For example:
Persuasive: "Investing in our new software will increase productivity by 30% and lead to cost savings."
Non-Persuasive: "Consider investing in our new software."

Remember practice and continuous improvement are key to developing strong business writing skills. Regularly reviewing and editing your work can help enhance clarity professionalism and effectiveness.

Here are 100 examples of business writing:

1. Business proposal for a new product launch.
   2. Sales pitch presentation to potential investors.
   3. Thank you email to a client after a successful meeting.
   4. Business plan for securing a loan from a financial institution.
   5. Letter of recommendation for an employee.
   6. Memorandum outlining new company policies.
   7. Press release announcing a new partnership.
   8. Employee handbook outlining company policies and procedures.
   9. Invoice for services rendered to a client.
   10. Job offer letter to a prospective employee.
   11. Performance review feedback for an employee.
   12. Letter of introduction to a potential business partner.
   13. Request for a meeting with a potential client.
   14. Complaint letter to a vendor about subpar product quality.
   15. Employee resignation letter.
   16. Conference invitation email with registration details.
   17. Proposal for a new marketing strategy.
   18. Thank you letter to a vendor for timely delivery of goods.
   19. Request for quote from a supplier for raw materials.
   20. Business case analysis for a potential investment opportunity.
   21. Announcement email for a company-wide event.
   22. Sales report presentation to the management team.
   23. Letter of intent to negotiate a partnership agreement.
   24. Request for a product demonstration from a supplier.
   25. Job application cover letter for a specific position.
   26. Company newsletter with updates on recent projects.
   27. Contract agreement for a new client engagement.
   28. Social media marketing campaign proposal.
   29. Meeting agenda for a team brainstorming session.
   30. Memo to employees regarding upcoming office renovations.

31. Follow-up email to a client after a sales meeting.

32. Product manual for customer usage instructions.

33. Request for a refund from a vendor for defective products.

34. Corporate social responsibility report outlining community initiatives.

35. Proposal for a new employee training program.

36. Notification email for a change in company leadership.

37. Business email introduction to a new client.

38. Request for a quote from a printing company for promotional materials.

39. Training manual for new employees.

40. Email reminder to employees about upcoming performance evaluations.

41. Request for a partnership opportunity with another company.

42. Sales forecast report for the upcoming quarter.

43. Announcement letter for a company rebranding.

44. Request for a price quote from a shipping carrier.

45. Job description for a newly created position within the organization.

46. Business email reminder about an overdue invoice payment.

47. Proposal for implementing a new employee benefits program.

48. Memo to employees regarding a change in the company's dress code.

49. Request for additional information from a potential vendor.

50. Product launch announcement for a new software release.

51. Customer satisfaction survey email to gather feedback.

52. Proposal for a new employee recognition program.

53. Announcement email for a company-wide charity event.

54. Request for a reference check for a potential employee.

55. Business report analyzing market trends and competition.

56. Thank you email to attendees after a successful company event.

57. Proposal for a company-wide cost-cutting initiative.

58. Memo to employees regarding a mandatory training session.

59. Request for a meeting with a government representative.

60. Social media content calendar for an upcoming marketing campaign.

61. Sales email to potential leads introducing a new product.

62. Proposal for a joint venture with another company.

63. Letter of agreement outlining terms and conditions for a business

partnership.

64. Request for a product sample from a supplier.

65. Job interview follow-up email to express gratitude for the opportunity.

66. Announcement email for a new employee joining the team.

67. Proposal for a new website redesign project.

68. Memo to employees regarding changes to the company's vacation policy.

69. Request for a product demonstration from a software vendor.

70. Request for a price negotiation from a service provider.

71. Business email reminder about an upcoming deadline for project submissions.

72. Proposal for implementing a new customer loyalty program.

73. Complaint letter to a utility provider about service disruptions.

74. Invitation letter to a networking event for industry professionals.

75. Sales presentation script for a client meeting.

76. Proposal for a company-wide sustainability initiative.

77. Memo to employees regarding updated safety protocols.

78. Request for a competitive analysis report from a market research company.

79. Job acceptance letter to confirm the offer and start date.

80. Announcement email for an employee recognition program.

81. Proposal for a new manufacturing process improvement.

82. Request for a product catalog from a supplier.

83. Business email reminder about an upcoming team meeting.

84. Thank you letter to a guest speaker at a company conference.

85. Proposal for a new sales training program.

86. Memo to employees regarding upcoming holiday office closures.

87. Request for a vendor performance review.

88. Complaint letter to a courier company about a lost shipment.

89. Request for a budget approval for a new project.

90. Business report analyzing financial performance and profitability.

91. Announcement email for a company-wide customer satisfaction survey.

92. Proposal for a new employee wellness program.

93. Memo to employees regarding a company-wide reorganization.

94. Request for a product demonstration from a machinery supplier.

95. Job rejection email to inform a candidate of the decision.

96. Sales email follow-up to prospects who showed interest but didn't convert.

97. Proposal for a new advertising campaign strategy.

98. Memo to employees regarding updated IT security protocols.

99. Request for a market research study on consumer behavior.

100. Business thank-you note to a client for their continued partnership.

These examples showcase the variety of business writing formats and purposes across different situations and contexts.

Emails and formal letters: Emails and formal letters are both forms of written communication but they differ in their format and level of formality.

Emails are electronic messages sent via the internet and are widely used for both personal and professional communication. They are often more informal than formal letters and are meant to be a quick and efficient means of communication. Emails typically have a subject line salutation body of the message and a closing. The tone of emails can vary depending on the relationship between the sender and recipient but generally they are more relaxed and conversational.

Formal letters on the other hand are written on paper or in a document format and are typically used for official or business communication. They are bound by certain conventions and follow a rigid structure. Formal letters usually begin with the sender's address the recipient's address a salutation body paragraphs and a closing. The tone of formal letters is typically more respectful and polite using formal language and avoiding contractions or slang.

Additionally formal letters often include specific elements such as a date reference or subject line and a signature. These elements make formal letters more official and suitable for business or legal purposes. Formal letters are also commonly used for job applications complaint letters requests or other official correspondence.

While both emails and formal letters serve the purpose of communication the choice between them depends on the context and purpose of the message. Emails are generally preferred for casual or time-sensitive conversations while formal letters are used for more official or important matters.

The format and examples of both emails and formal letters.

Emails:
   Format:
   1. Subject line: This is a brief summary of the content of the email.

2. Salutation: Begin the email with a polite greeting like "Dear [Recipient's Name]".

3. Introduction: Start the email by introducing yourself and the purpose of the email.

4. Body: Provide the main content or information in a clear and concise manner. Use paragraphs to organize your thoughts and make it easier to read.

5. Closing: End the email with a polite closing like "Regards" or "Sincerely".

6. Signature: Include your name job title and contact information at the end of the email.

Example:

Subject: Inquiry about job vacancy

Dear Mr. JohnsonI hope this email finds you well. My name is Alice Thompson and I am writing to inquire about any job vacancies at your company ABC Corp. I recently came across your company's website and was impressed by your values and accomplishments.

I have a bachelor's degree in Business Administration and three years of experience in a similar role. I am particularly interested in the sales and marketing department and believe my skills and experience align well with the requirements stated in the job posting.

I have attached my resume for your reference. I would greatly appreciate it if you could review my qualifications and let me know if there are any opportunities available.

Thank you for your time and consideration. I look forward to hearing from you soon.

RegardsAlice Thompson
   Sales and Marketing Professional
   Email: alice.thompson@email.com
   Phone: +123456789

Formal Letters:
   Format:
   1. Your address: Include your full name address and contact information at the top.

2. Date: Write the date when the letter is being written.

3. Recipient's address: Include the full name designation and address of the recipient below your address.

4. Salutation: Begin the letter with a formal greeting like "Dear Mr. Smith" or "Dear Mrs. Johnson".

5. Introduction: Start the letter by introducing yourself and the purpose of the letter.

6. Body: Provide the main content or information in a clear and organized manner. Use paragraphs to separate different points.

7. Closing: End the letter with a polite closing like "Yours sincerely" or "Best regards".

8. Signature: Sign your name below the closing and include your job title if applicable.

Example:

Alice Thompson
    123 Main Street
    City State ZIP Code
    Email: alice.thompson@email.com
    Phone: +123456789

Date: March 15 2021

Mr. John Smith
    Human Resources Manager
    ABC Corp
    456 Park Avenue
    City State ZIP Code

Dear Mr. SmithI am writing to formally apply for the position of Sales Representative at ABC Corp as advertised on your company's website. I have been working in the sales industry for five years and believe that my skills and experience make me a strong candidate for the role.

During my previous employment at XYZ Company I consistently achieved and exceeded sales targets by implementing effective sales strategies and building strong relationships with clients. Furthermore I have a strong understanding of your industry and am confident in my ability to contribute to the sales team at ABC Corp.

I have enclosed my resume which provides further details about my qualifications and achievements. I would greatly appreciate it if you could review my application and consider me for the position. I am available for an interview at your convenience.

Thank you for considering my application. I look forward to hearing from you soon.

Yours sincerelyAlice Thompson
    Sales and Marketing Professional

Reports and memos : Reports and memos are both important forms of business writing that serve different purposes and cater to specific audiences within an organization.

Reports are typically longer more formal documents that provide detailed information and analysis on a particular topic or issue. They are often used to inform decision-making document research findings or provide updates on projects or initiatives. Reports are typically organized with sections such as an introduction methodology results analysis and conclusions. They are often supported with data and evidence and are written in a formal tone.

For example a financial report may be prepared by an accountant to provide the management team with an overview of the company's financial performance including revenue expenses and profitability. The report may analyze trends identify areas of concern and make recommendations for improvement.

On the other hand memos (or memorandums) are shorter more concise documents used for internal communication within an organization. They are typically used to convey information make announcements request action or provide updates. Memos are less formal and usually written in a more conversational tone.

For example an office manager may send a memo to all employees to inform them about an upcoming company-wide meeting. The memo may provide the date time and location of the meeting as well as any relevant details or expectations. It may also remind employees to come prepared with any necessary materials or information.

Overall reports and memos are written for different purposes and audiences but both serve important communication functions within a business setting. Reports provide detailed analysis and information for decision-making while memos are used for more informal and internal communication.

Speaking and Listening Skills

English speaking and listening skills are essential components of effective communication in English. Speaking skills refer to the ability to express oneself fluently and accurately in spoken English while listening skills refer to the ability to understand and comprehend spoken English.

To develop English speaking skills it is important to practice speaking regularly. This can be done by engaging in conversations with native English speakers participating in group discussions or debates or even speaking to oneself in front of a mirror. It is also beneficial to listen to English speakers and mimic their pronunciation intonation and word usage. Additionally expanding one's vocabulary and knowledge of grammar rules can help improve speaking confidence and accuracy.

On the other hand to develop English listening skills it is necessary to actively listen to spoken English and make a conscious effort to understand. This can be achieved by regularly listening to English audio materials such as podcasts news broadcasts or songs. It is also helpful to watch English movies or TV shows with subtitles to improve comprehension. Taking notes while listening and practicing summarizing what was heard can also enhance listening skills.

Improving both speaking and listening skills requires regular practice and exposure to the English language. Engaging in conversation with native speakers or joining English language groups can provide valuable opportunities to practice and receive feedback. It is important to be patient and persistent in developing these skills as it takes time and effort to become proficient.

Effective phone etiquette : Effective phone etiquette is important in maintaining professional and polite communication with others. It involves using proper manners and practices when answering making and ending phone calls.

Here are 100 examples of effective phone etiquette:

1. Answer calls promptly.
2. Greet the caller with a warm and professional tone.
3. Identify yourself and your organization.
4. Use phrases like "Good morning/afternoon/evening" and "How may I help you?"
5. Speak clearly and enunciate your words.
6. Use proper grammar and avoid slang or jargon.
7. Avoid interrupting the caller while they are speaking.
8. Be patient and listen attentively to the caller.
9. Use appropriate volume – neither too loud nor too soft.
10. Avoid chewing gum or eating while on a call.
11. Avoid typing or engaging in other activities that may create noise during a call.
12. Stay focused on the conversation and avoid distractions.
13. Ask for clarification if you didn't understand something.
14. Take notes to remember important details discussed during the call.
15. If you need to transfer the call inform the caller beforehand and get their permission.
16. Provide the caller with accurate information and solutions.
17. Be proactive in offering assistance or directing the caller to the appropriate person or department.
18. Avoid putting callers on hold for extended periods without their consent.

19. If putting someone on hold inform them about the estimated wait time.

20. Ask permission before placing a caller on hold.

21. Offer to take a message if the person the caller is seeking is unavailable.

22. Avoid sounding bored irritated or rude.

23. Use positive and polite language throughout the conversation.

24. Be empathetic and understanding towards the caller's concerns.

25. Apologize if there is a mistake or misunderstanding on your end.

26. Avoid speaking negatively about colleagues or clients during a call.

27. Minimize background noise by finding a quiet environment for phone calls.

28. Speak at a moderate pace to allow the caller to follow along easily.

29. Use proper phone etiquette even when leaving voicemail messages.

30. Keep voicemail messages concise and clear.

31. Repeat your name and phone number when leaving a voicemail message.

32. Return missed calls promptly.

33. Avoid using a speakerphone unless necessary.

34. Speak directly into the phone's microphone for better sound quality.

35. Keep personal conversations private and separate from work-related calls.

36. Avoid personal interruptions or distractions during work calls.

37. Thank the caller for their time and cooperation.

38. End the call with a sincere goodbye.

39. Hang up the phone gently to avoid abruptly disconnecting the call.

40. Avoid making calls during inappropriate or inconvenient hours.

41. Always respect the caller's privacy and confidentiality.

42. Develop a pleasant and professional tone of voice.

43. Use appropriate greetings based on the time of day.

44. Address the caller by their name if known.

45. Be mindful of cultural differences and adjust your communication style accordingly.

46. Avoid lengthy silences during a call as it may make the caller feel disconnected.

47. Practice active listening by paraphrasing and reflecting what the caller

said.

48. Stay calm and composed even if the caller seems upset or angry.

49. Control your emotions and avoid getting defensive.

50. Use positive language when offering solutions or alternatives to the caller.

51. Do not engage in personal conversations or use informal language.

52. Always introduce yourself when making calls.

53. Clearly state the purpose of your call.

54. Prepare in advance for important calls by organizing necessary information.

55. Avoid multitasking during a call.

56. Be aware of your tone and inflection as it can convey different meanings.

57. Keep your conversation on track and avoid going off topic.

58. Speak slowly and articulate your words when leaving information like phone numbers or addresses.

59. Confirm important details with the caller to avoid misunderstandings.

60. Do not use excessive or unnecessary jargon during a call.

61. Do not speak too close to the microphone as it may distort the sound.

62. Avoid talking over the caller or interrupting them.

63. If you are expecting a call try to answer it within the first few rings.

64. Avoid using your phone in noisy environments to ensure clear communication.

65. If you need to place a caller on hold make sure to regularly update them on the status.

66. Respect the caller's time by providing prompt and efficient assistance.

67. Avoid asking personal or intrusive questions during a call.

68. Do not use your phone to talk or text while in a meeting or social gathering.

69. If you need to end a call abruptly apologize and explain the reason.

70. If you need to escalate a call to a manager or supervisor inform the caller about the process.

71. Always follow company guidelines and policies related to phone etiquette.

72. Avoid shouting or raising your voice during a call even if the caller

becomes confrontational.

73. Avoid using slang or informal language even if you have a friendly relationship with the caller.

74. Be mindful of your tone and voice level when speaking with elderly or hearing-impaired individuals.

75. Use appropriate call-waiting features if available to avoid keeping the caller waiting for too long.

76. Avoid having personal conversations or discussing confidential matters in public areas where others can overhear.

77. Be aware of your body language even though the caller cannot see you.

78. Avoid using your phone while driving as it can be dangerous and distracting.

79. If you are not sure how to handle a caller's request ask a colleague or supervisor for guidance.

80. Be patient with callers who may have difficulty understanding or communicating due to language barriers.

81. Avoid excessive use of filler words like "um" or "ah" during the call.

82. Be respectful and considerate when asking the caller for personal information.

83. Use proper phone etiquette when leaving a message on an answering machine.

84. Avoid using your phone during important face-to-face interactions or meetings.

85. Be mindful of your phone's battery life to avoid unexpected disconnections during calls.

86. Do not use your phone during bathroom breaks or in other inappropriate locations.

87. Adapt your communication style based on the caller's level of familiarity or formality.

88. If the caller becomes abusive or aggressive remain calm and professional.

89. Seek feedback from colleagues or supervisors on your phone etiquette to continually improve.

90. Avoid placing a call on speakerphone without informing the other party.

91. Use a professional and personalized voicemail greeting on your phone.

92. Avoid using slang or technical jargon that the caller may not understand.

93. Do not interrupt the caller when they are providing details or explanations.

94. Provide a direct extension or contact information for the caller to reach you if needed.

95. Speak slowly and clearly when leaving a callback number on voicemail.

96. Be proactive in resolving the caller's issue or concern even if it requires follow-up action.

97. Avoid discussing personal or confidential information about the caller with others.

98. Use appropriate language and terminology based on the industry or field you are working in.

99. If the caller needs to be transferred to another department inform them and provide clear instructions.

100. Always end the call on a positive note thanking the caller for their time and cooperation.

These examples highlight the key principles of effective phone etiquette and can be applied in various professional settings to ensure clear and courteous communication over the phone.

Presenting confidently and engagingly : Presenting confidently and engagingly is an essential skill that can captivate and persuade an audience. It involves not only delivering information effectively but also ensuring that your audience remains interested and involved throughout the presentation. Here are some key strategies and examples to help you excel in your presentations.

1. Know your audience: Understanding your audience's background interests and needs can help you tailor your content and delivery to their preferences. For example if you are presenting to a group of professionals in a specific industry you can use industry-specific terminology and examples to make

your presentation more relatable and engaging.

2. Start with a captivating opening: Begin your presentation with a strong opening that grabs your audience's attention and sets the tone for the rest of the presentation. You can use a relevant story a surprising statistic or a thought-provoking question. For instance if you are giving a presentation on the importance of renewable energy you can start by sharing a personal experience of witnessing the negative impacts of fossil fuels.

3. Use visuals and multimedia: Incorporating visuals such as slides images videos and info graphics can significantly enhance your presentation's impact. Visual aids can help clarify complex concepts provide context and keep your audience engaged. For example if you are presenting data on the growth of e-commerce you can use a graph or chart to visually illustrate the upward trend.

4. Develop a clear and logical structure: Organize your presentation in a logical manner so that your message is easy to follow. Use headings subheadings and bullet points to help your audience navigate through the content. Additionally make sure your transitions between different sections or topics are smooth and coherent guiding your audience seamlessly through your presentation.

5. Use storytelling techniques: Incorporate storytelling elements to humanize your presentation and make it more relatable. For example you can share personal anecdotes case studies or success stories to illustrate your main points. A story can engage your audience emotionally making them more invested in your presentation.

6. Use a confident and enthusiastic delivery: Your body language tone of voice and facial expressions contribute to how well your presentation is received. Maintain good eye contact with your audience use gestures effectively and vary your tone to convey enthusiasm and confidence. A confident and engaging delivery can captivate your audience and make your presentation

more memorable.

7. Encourage interaction and participation: Engage your audience by encouraging them to participate actively during the presentation. You can ask rhetorical questions facilitate discussions or conduct short activities. For example if you are giving a presentation on team building you can ask the audience to share their experiences or ideas for effective teamwork.

8. Practice and prepare thoroughly: Confidence comes from practice and preparedness. Rehearse your presentation multiple times to familiarize yourself with the content and flow. Anticipate questions or potential challenges that may arise and be prepared with well-thought-out responses. The more prepared you are the more confidently and engagingly you can present.

By incorporating these strategies into your presentations you can enhance your ability to present confidently and engagingly. Remember a well-presented message has the power to inform inspire and influence your audience effectively.

II

Business Communication Strategies

"Business Communication Strategies" unveils the art of persuasive corporate discourse. Discover the lexicon of meetings, negotiations, and discussions, empowering you to articulate opinions and clinch agreements. With insights into virtual communication challenges and cultural barriers, this segment equips you to navigate diverse scenarios with finesse.

Business Meetings and Negotiations

Business meetings and negotiations are common in the world of business and are essential for making important decisions closing deals and establishing partnerships. These meetings play a crucial role in shaping the future of a company and its relationships with other organizations.

Here are a few examples of business meetings and negotiations:

1. Sales Negotiation: A sales negotiation is a process where parties try to reach an agreement on the terms of a sale. For example a salesperson may negotiate with a potential customer over the price quantity and delivery schedule of a product. The objective is to find a mutually beneficial solution that satisfies both parties' needs.

2. Partnership Meeting: When two companies are considering entering into a partnership they often hold meetings to discuss the terms and conditions of the agreement. This could include discussing areas of collaboration revenue sharing intellectual property rights and overall business strategies. The aim is to reach an agreement that benefits both organizations and paves the way for a successful partnership.

3. Board Meeting: Board meetings are gatherings where the directors of a company come together to make important decisions about the organization's future. These meetings often involve reviewing financial reports discussing strategic plans and approving major investments or acquisitions. Board

meetings require effective communication collaboration and negotiation skills to ensure all opinions are considered before a decision is made.

4. Employee Performance Review: Performance reviews are a form of business meeting where managers assess the performance of their employees and provide feedback. During these meetings goals are typically set performance is evaluated and any necessary adjustments to duties or expectations are discussed. Negotiation may occur when discussing areas for improvement or negotiating salary increases or promotions.

5. Supplier Negotiation: Businesses frequently negotiate with their suppliers to obtain better pricing delivery terms or quality standards for the materials or services they require. For example a manufacturer may negotiate with a supplier to lower the cost of raw materials or lengthen payment terms. These negotiations aim to find a win-win solution that benefits both parties while maintaining a strong supplier-client relationship.

In conclusion business meetings and negotiations are crucial for making important decisions closing deals and building successful relationships. They require effective communication collaboration and negotiation skills to reach mutually beneficial outcomes.

Vocabulary for meetings and negotiations :

Here are 100 vocabulary words and phrases commonly used in meetings and negotiations:

1. Agenda - A list of topics to be discussed in a meeting.
   2. Chairperson - The person who leads the meeting.
   3. Minute taker - The person responsible for recording the minutes of the

meeting.

4. Action item - A task or action that needs to be completed.

5. Proposal - A suggestion or plan put forward for consideration.

6. Objective - The goal or purpose of the meeting or negotiation.

7. Attendee - A person who is present at the meeting.

8. Break the ice - To initiate conversation or create a relaxed atmosphere.

9. Introduction - A brief opening statement or self-introduction.

10. Recap - To summarize or give a brief overview of what has been discussed.

11. Point of order - A question or concern about the proper procedure of the meeting.

12. Conflict resolution - Finding a solution to disagreements or conflicts.

13. Consensus - Agreement among all participants.

14. Decision-making - The process of reaching a conclusion or making a choice.

15. Brainstorming - A group activity to generate creative ideas.

16. Feedback - Constructive criticism or suggestions given to improve something.

17. Deadline - The date by which something needs to be completed.

18. Follow-up - To contact after the meeting to provide additional information or updates.

19. Negotiation - The process of discussing terms and reaching a compromise.

20. Concession - A compromise or giving up something in negotiations.

21. Counter proposal - A response to a proposal offering an alternative solution.

22. Win-win - A solution that benefits both parties in a negotiation.

23. Bottom line - The most important or essential factor.

24. Mediation - The process of resolving a dispute with the help of a neutral third party.

25. Deadlock - A situation where no progress or agreement can be reached.

26. Trade-off - Giving up something in exchange for gaining something else.

27. Impasse – A point where no agreement can be reached.

28. Memorandum of understanding (MOU) – A document outlining a tentative agreement.

29. Non-disclosure agreement (NDA) – An agreement to protect confidential information.

30. Terms and conditions – Specific requirements rules or criteria.

31. Contract – A legally binding agreement between parties.

32. Clarification – Seeking further explanation or understanding on a point.

33. Objection – A protest or disagreement regarding a proposal or decision.

34. Resolution – A formal decision or action taken to resolve an issue.

35. Quorum – The minimum number of attendees required for a meeting to be valid.

36. Off the record – Information not to be officially recorded or used.

37. Rapport – A positive and harmonious relationship between people.

38. Compromise – Finding a middle ground or settling differences.

39. Consistency – Doing something in a similar manner over time.

40. Prioritize – To determine the order of importance or urgency.

41. Progress report – An update on the status of a project or task.

42. Stakeholder – A person or group with an interest in the outcomes of a project or negotiation.

43. Collaborate – To work together with others towards a common goal.

44. Reschedule – To change the date or time of a meeting.

45. Oversee – To supervise or be in charge of something.

46. Mitigate – To reduce or lessen the severity of an issue.

47. Present – To share or deliver information in a meeting.

48. Validate – To confirm or support the validity or accuracy of something.

49. Consensus-building – The process of working towards agreement.

50. Icebreaker – An activity or question to initiate conversation and build relationships.

51. Facilitator – A person who helps guide and manage the meeting process.

52. Scope – The range or extent of a project or discussion.

53. Memorandum – A written record or communication summarizing important information.

54. Quota – A specific target or goal to be achieved.

55. Impartial – Neutral or unbiased; not favoring any particular side.

56. Recapitulate – To summarize or restate the main points.

57. Ratify – To officially approve or confirm a decision or agreement.

58. Turnover – The rate at which people leave or are replaced in a company.

59. Tenure – The length of time someone holds a particular position or role.

60. Preamble – An introductory statement or explanation.

61. Contingency plan – A backup plan in case the original plan fails.

62. Ground rules – Specific guidelines or principles for behavior and conduct in the meeting.

63. Moot point – A point of discussion that is no longer relevant or debatable.

64. Option – A choice or alternative course of action.

65. Protocol – The official procedures or rules for conducting a meeting.

66. Silent majority – People who hold a particular opinion but do not express it.

67. Interim – Temporary or provisional; in the meantime.

68. On the same page – Being in agreement or understanding a concept.

69. Win-lose – A negotiation outcome where one party gains at the expense of the other.

70. Deal breaker – A term or condition that is unacceptable and would cause negotiations to end.

71. Power dynamics – The distribution of power and influence among individuals or groups.

72. Walk away – To terminate negotiations and leave without reaching an agreement.

73. Draft – To create a preliminary version of a document or agreement.

74. Redline – To mark changes or edits on a document.

75. Scheduling conflict – A situation where two or more events or activities occur at the same time.

76. Consensus-driven – A decision-making process that involves reaching agreement among all parties.

77. Performance review – An evaluation of an individual's or group's performance.

78. Critical path - The sequence of tasks that must be completed for a project to be finished on time.

79. Contention - A disagreement or conflict between parties.

80. Bureaucracy - Excessive rules or procedures that hinder efficiency.

81. Remuneration - Compensation or payment for services or work.

82. Sanction - An official authorization or approval.

83. Comprise - To include or contain; to be made up of.

84. Mandate - An official order or authorization to take a particular action.

85. Stalemate - A deadlock or situation in which no progress can be made.

86. Trust-building - Activities or efforts aimed at fostering trust among participants.

87. Protocol - Formal etiquette or rules for behavior in a particular setting.

88. Quota - A specific target or goal to be met or achieved.

89. Sideline - To exclude or remove someone from a process or discussion.

90. Collaboration - Working together to achieve a common goal.

91. Streamline - To make a process more efficient by removing unnecessary steps.

92. Consensus-driven - A decision-making process that involves reaching agreement among all parties.

93. On the table - A proposal or option that is currently being discussed.

94. Status update - A report on the current progress or situation.

95. Endorse - To give support or approval to a proposal or idea.

96. Optimize - To make the best or most effective use of something.

97. Confidentiality - The protection and non-disclosure of sensitive information.

98. Dispute - A disagreement or argument between two parties.

99. Impartial - Neutral or unbiased; not favoring any particular side.

100. Adjourn - To officially end or postpone a meeting.

These vocabulary words and phrases should help you navigate and participate effectively in both meetings and negotiations.

Participating in discussions and expressing opinions :

Participating in discussions and expressing opinions is an important aspect of communication and social interaction. It allows individuals to share their thoughts ideas and perspectives on various topics and issues. By actively engaging in discussions individuals can contribute to the exchange of information promote critical thinking and help create a more informed and inclusive dialogue.

Expressing opinions in discussions involves sharing personal viewpoints and beliefs on a particular subject matter. This can be done through verbal communication written statements or even non-verbal cues such as body language and facial expressions. By articulating their opinions individuals can contribute to the diversity of ideas and perspectives within a group fostering a more well-rounded and comprehensive understanding of the issue at hand.

Engaging in discussions and expressing opinions can have several benefits. It allows individuals to develop and refine their own ideas and arguments through the process of defending and justifying their opinions. It also provides opportunities for individuals to learn from others gain new insights and broaden their understanding of different viewpoints. Additionally discussions can challenge preconceived notions evoke critical thinking and promote intellectual growth and personal development.

However it is important to approach discussions and the expression of opinions with respect and open-mindedness. It is essential to listen to others even if their opinions differ from our own and engage in constructive dialogue rather than engaging in personal attacks or dismissing opposing viewpoints. By fostering a respectful and inclusive environment discussions can become platforms for constructive debate and collaboration.

Negotiating and reaching agreements :

Negotiating is the process of seeking a mutually beneficial outcome through communication and compromise. It involves discussing and finding an agreement on issues or terms that both parties involved find acceptable.

Reaching agreements is the end goal of negotiation where both parties have agreed to specific terms and conditions. These agreements can be in various contexts such as business deals personal relationships or diplomatic treaties.

Here are some examples of negotiating and reaching agreements:

1. Salary negotiation: When a person is offered a job they may negotiate their salary with the employer to reach an agreement on the amount they will be paid. This negotiation can involve discussing factors like experience qualifications and market rates to reach a fair agreement.

2. International trade agreements: Countries negotiate trade deals to establish favorable terms for both parties involved. For example the North American Free Trade Agreement (NAFTA) was a negotiated agreement between Canada Mexico and the United States to eliminate trade barriers and establish fair competition.

3. Divorce settlement: During divorce proceedings couples negotiate and reach agreements on issues like child custody alimony and the division of assets. Both parties may have different interests and needs and the negotiation process aims to find a compromise that meets the best interests of all involved.

4. Business partnerships: When forming a business partnership individuals negotiate various terms and conditions such as the roles and responsibilities of each partner profit-sharing arrangements and decision-making processes. The negotiation process helps establish a clear agreement on how the part-

nership will operate.

5. Diplomatic agreements: In international relations countries negotiate and reach agreements on various issues such as peace treaties nuclear disarmament and climate change. These negotiations involve compromises and concessions from both sides to establish mutually beneficial agreements.

Overall negotiation and reaching agreements are essential skills in various aspects of life. It requires effective communication understanding the needs and interests of all parties involved and finding a solution that satisfies everyone to achieve successful outcomes.

Teleconferences and Video conferences

English teleconferences and video conferences are forms of communication that allow individuals or groups to participate in meetings or discussions remotely without having to be physically present in the same location. These types of conferences provide opportunities for effective communication and collaboration with teams clients or stakeholders located in different parts of the world.

In an English teleconference participants use phone lines or audio conferencing software to communicate with each other. They can dial in to a designated phone number or use Voice over Internet Protocol (VoIP) services. This method is ideal for simple discussions or updates where visual aids or physical presence is not necessary.

For example a team of English language teachers from different schools might have a teleconference to discuss curriculum development. They can share their ideas exchange resources and provide feedback to each other without the need for extensive travel or face-to-face meetings.

On the other hand English video conferences involve the use of webcams video conferencing software or platforms like Zoom Microsoft Teams or Skype. This allows participants to not only hear but also see each other during the meeting. Video conferences are especially effective for more interactive discussions presentations or collaborative work that requires visual aids gestures or facial expressions.

For instance an international business team might conduct a video conference to discuss a new product launch. The team can give presentations show product prototypes share relevant documents or screens and engage in real-time discussion with visual cues. This helps to foster a more immersive and productive communication experience despite being geographically dispersed.

English teleconferences and video conferences are particularly valuable in today's globalized world. They save time and costs associated with travel while still allowing for effective communication and collaboration. These methods enable individuals or teams to work together efficiently regardless of their physical locations promoting more efficient and inclusive business practices.

Preparing for virtual meetings & Managing audio and visual communication

Preparing for virtual meetings involves several steps to ensure smooth communication and collaboration. Here are some key steps to consider:

1. Test your equipment: Make sure your computer or device is properly set up for virtual meetings. Test your microphone speakers or headphones and webcam to ensure they are working correctly. If necessary update your software or download any required plugins for the meeting platform.

2. Choose the right meeting platform: There are several virtual meeting platforms available such as Zoom Microsoft Teams Google Meet and Skype. Familiarize yourself with the platform that will be used for the meeting and ensure you have the necessary login credentials.

3. Check your internet connection: A strong and stable internet connection is

crucial for virtual meetings. Test your internet speed and consider connecting to a wired network if possible to avoid any disruptions in the meeting.

4. Find a suitable location: Set up your workspace in a quiet area with minimal distractions. Make sure the lighting is adequate and there are no strong background noises that can interfere with the meeting.

5. Dress appropriately: Treat virtual meetings like in-person meetings and dress professionally. This helps to maintain a level of professionalism and respect for the meeting participants.

6. Prepare your agenda and materials: Just like a physical meeting virtual meetings benefit from having a clear agenda. Share any necessary documents or presentations with the meeting participants in advance to review and refer to during the meeting.

7. Establish meeting etiquette: Communicating effectively in a virtual meeting requires establishing some ground rules. Remind participants to mute themselves when not speaking to minimize background noise. Encourage everyone to use the raise hand feature or chat function to indicate they have something to contribute.

8. Manage audio and visual communication: In virtual meetings audio and visual communication play a crucial role. Make sure your microphone is working properly and speak clearly and audibly. Pay attention to non-verbal cues and maintain eye contact with the webcam to engage with other participants. It's also important to manage the video aspect by ensuring proper lighting and framing the camera appropriately.

9. Optimize meeting settings: Familiarize yourself with the features of the meeting platform you are using. This includes knowing how to share your screen use the chat function mute and unmute yourself and manage participant settings.

10. Engage actively in the meeting: Stay engaged and actively participate in the meeting by listening attentively providing input and asking questions. Avoid multitasking or being distracted by other devices during the meeting.

By following these steps you can ensure that you are well-prepared for virtual meetings and can effectively communicate and collaborate with others.

Overcoming challenges in virtual communication

Overcoming challenges in virtual communication can be a complex task as it requires adapting to a different form of communication that lacks the physical presence and immediate feedback found in face-to-face interactions. However with the right strategies it is possible to navigate and excel in virtual communication.

One of the first challenges to overcome in virtual communication is the potential for misinterpretation. Without visual and nonverbal cues messages can be easily misconstrued leading to misunderstandings and conflict. Therefore it is crucial to be clear and concise in communication using appropriate vocabulary and avoiding ambiguous language.

Building rapport and fostering a sense of connection is another challenge in virtual communication. Without the ability to have informal conversations or engage in small talk it can be difficult to establish trust and build relationships. However using empathy and active listening can help bridge this gap and create a sense of camaraderie.

Another hurdle in virtual communication is the lack of immediate feedback. In face-to-face conversations we can gauge the reaction and understanding of the other person through their facial expressions and body language. In a virtual setting this feedback may be delayed or nonexistent making it necessary to ask for clarification and actively seek feedback to ensure effective communication.

Technology-related challenges such as technical difficulties or poor audio/video quality can also hinder virtual communication. It is essential to be prepared and familiar with the technology being used as well as to have backup plans in case of technical glitches. Patience and adaptability are key in these situations.

100 vocabulary words used in overcoming challenges in virtual communication:

1. Adaptability
2. Ambiguous
3. Camaraderie
4. Clarity
5. Communication
6. Complex
7. Conflict
8. Connection
9. Delayed
10. Difficulties
11. Effectiveness
12. Empathy
13. Establish
14. Excel
15. Feedback
16. Form
17. Foster

18. Gaps
19. Glitches
20. Immediate
21. Informal
22. Interactions
23. Lack
24. Language
25. Listen
26. Misconstrued
27. Misinterpretation
28. Navigating
29. Nonverbal
30. Patience
31. Physical
32. Potential
33. Preparing
34. Presence
35. Quality
36. Rapport
37. Reaction
38. Relationships
39. Sense
40. Setting
41. Small talk
42. Strategies
43. Task
44. Technology
45. Trust
46. Understanding
47. Vocabulary
48. Virtual
49. Aggressive
50. Amicable

51. Assertive
52. Assumptions
53. Collaboration
54. Cooperation
55. Cultural differences
56. Disagreements
57. Distractions
58. Equivocal
59. Etiquette
60. Expressions
61. Face-to-face
62. Formalities
63. Images
64. Impersonal
65. Inclusivity
66. Interpersonal
67. Interruptions
68. Manners
69. Mediation
70. Multitasking
71. Nervousness
72. norms
73. Open-mindedness
74. Overload
75. Paraphrasing
76. Patience
77. Politeness
78. Prejudice
79. Productivity
80. Proficiency
81. Reciprocity
82. Responsiveness
83. Shared meaning

84. Simplicity
85. Social cues
86. Stereotypes
87. Stress
88. Summarizing
89. Synchronous
90. Task-oriented
91. Tension
92. Time zones
93. Tone
94. Unconscious bias
95. Unreliable
96. Video conferencing
97. Webinars
98. Welcoming
99. Wire frames
100. Workplace

Business Presentations

Business presentations are formal presentations that are delivered in a professional setting to convey information persuade or influence an audience. These presentations are commonly used in various business contexts such as sales pitches investor meetings team meetings and internal or external company presentations.

The main purpose of a business presentation is to communicate a message effectively and engage the audience. It typically involves creating and delivering a visually appealing presentation using multimedia tools such as slides charts graphs and videos. However the content and format of a business presentation may vary depending on the specific objective and audience.

To create a compelling business presentation it is important to carefully plan and structure the content. This includes identifying the main message or purpose of the presentation organizing the information logically and selecting the most relevant and impactful visuals. The content of the presentation should be clear concise and well-supported with relevant data or evidence.

Delivery skills are also crucial in business presentations. The presenter should be confident engaging and able to effectively communicate with the audience. This includes using appropriate body language maintaining eye contact speaking clearly and confidently and adapting the delivery style to suit the audience's needs and preferences.

In addition to the content and delivery a business presentation should also consider the design and aesthetics of the slides. This includes using a consistent and visually pleasing color scheme selecting appropriate fonts and incorporating relevant visuals or graphics to enhance the overall appeal and understanding of the presentation.

Business presentations can also incorporate interactive elements to increase engagement and participation. This can include asking questions inviting the audience to share their thoughts or experiences and using interactive tools or technologies to create a dynamic and memorable presentation experience.

Organizing and structuring a presentation involves creating a logical flow of information and arranging it in a way that best communicates the message to the audience. This can be done through various techniques such as creating an outline or using a clear introduction body and conclusion format.

Example:
   Let's say you are giving a presentation on the benefits of exercise. You could organize your presentation in the following way:

Introduction:
   - Greet the audience and introduce yourself.
   - Explain the importance of exercise and why it is relevant to the audience.
   - State the main purpose and objectives of the presentation.

Body:
   - Start by discussing the physical benefits of exercise such as improved cardiovascular health increased strength and weight management.
   - Move on to the mental benefits such as reduced stress improved mood and increased cognitive function.
   - Discuss the social benefits such as building relationships and promoting teamwork.

- Provide examples and statistics to support your claims.

- Use clear and concise subheadings to divide the information into sections and ensure a smooth transition between topics.

Conclusion:

- Summarize the main points discussed in the body of the presentation.

- Reinforce the importance of exercise and how it can positively impact one's life.

- End with a memorable closing statement or call to action.

Using visual aids effectively can enhance a presentation by providing visual representation of information and helping the audience better understand and remember key points. Examples of visual aids include PowerPoint slides diagrams charts graphs and videos.

Example:

Continuing with the exercise benefits presentation you could use visual aids such as:

- A chart comparing the physical benefits of exercise before and after a certain period of consistent workout.

- Images of people engaging in different types of exercises demonstrating the variety and versatility of exercise options.

- A graph showing the correlation between exercise frequency and stress levels.

- A video testimonial of someone who experienced significant weight loss and improved health through regular exercise.

Delivering a compelling and persuasive presentation involves engaging the audience and effectively conveying your message to convince them to adopt your perspective or take a specific action. This can be achieved through various techniques such as using storytelling incorporating persuasive language and connecting emotionally with the audience.

Example:

During the exercise benefits presentation you could:

- Share a personal anecdote about how exercise has positively impacted your own life making it relatable and engaging for the audience. For example you could talk about how exercise helped you overcome a stressful period and achieve a healthier lifestyle.

- Use strong and persuasive language to highlight the importance and benefits of exercise. For instance you could say "Exercise is not just an option it is a necessity for a happy and healthy life. Don't wait another day to start investing in your well-being."

- Frame the presentation around the audience's needs and desires. For example instead of simply stating the physical benefits of exercise emphasize how these benefits can help them improve their performance at work or have more energy to spend quality time with their loved ones.

Vocabulary:

- Outline: a plan or summary of the main points or components of something.

- Introduction: the opening part of a presentation where the speaker introduces the topic and purpose.

- Body: the main part of a presentation where the speaker provides detailed information and supports their argument or point of view.

- Conclusion: the closing part of a presentation where the speaker summarizes the main points and often provides a final thought or call to action.

- Visual aids: objects images or media used to visually support or enhance a presentation.

- Persuasive: convincing or causing someone to believe or do something through reasoning or argument.

- Anecdote: a brief personal story or account that illustrates a specific point.

- Persuasive language: language that is designed to influence or change the opinions or actions of others.

- Emotional connection: establishing a personal or emotional bond with the audience to create engagement and empathy.

Overall a successful business presentation requires careful planning effective communication and engaging delivery. By effectively conveying the intended message and engaging the audience business presentations can be a powerful tool for conveying information influencing decisions and driving business success.

Networking and Socializing in a Business Setting

Networking and socializing in a business setting are essential activities for professionals looking to build relationships expand their contacts and enhance their professional opportunities. These activities involve engaging with others in industry-related events conferences meetings and social gatherings to establish connections exchange information and foster collaboration.

Networking refers to the process of forming and maintaining professional relationships with individuals who may be beneficial to one's career or business. It involves actively engaging with others such as colleagues clients business partners and industry leaders to build rapport share information and leverage mutual interests and goals. Networking can be a powerful tool for accessing new job opportunities business leads partnerships and mentorship.

To effectively network in a business setting it is crucial to have strong interpersonal skills such as active listening effective communication and the ability to establish a genuine connection. Networking events provide an opportunity to meet people face-to-face exchange business cards and engage in meaningful conversations. Staying in touch with contacts through professional networking platforms such as LinkedIn further strengthens relationships and keeps the lines of communication open.

Socializing in a business setting refers to the interaction and engagement with others beyond the formal boundaries of work-related activities. It involves attending social events such as company parties industry gatherings and after-work functions where professionals can relax unwind and establish more personal connections. Socializing provides a more casual environment for professionals to get to know each other on a personal level build trust and foster camaraderie.

While networking focuses on professional connections socializing allows individuals to bond and create a sense of community. It is an opportunity to showcase one's personality interests and hobbies outside of the workplace which can help strengthen relationships and create a more supportive and collaborative work environment. Socializing also contributes to a positive company culture as it encourages teamwork boosts morale and improves overall job satisfaction.

Both networking and socializing in a business setting require a proactive approach and strategic planning. Setting clear goals identifying key individuals to connect with and being prepared with a well-crafted elevator pitch or talking points can help professionals make the most of these opportunities. It is important to be sincere genuine and respectful during interactions focusing on building mutually beneficial relationships rather than simply seeking personal gains.

1. Icebreakers and small talk:
   Icebreakers and small talk are essential in networking as they help people establish a comfortable and friendly atmosphere. Icebreakers are conversation starters that are used to initiate a discussion or engage with someone. They can be simple questions like "How did you hear about this event?" or "What brings you here today?" Small talk refers to light and casual conversations such as discussing current events hobbies or common interests.

Example:

Person A: "Hi I'm John. Have you attended this conference before?"

Person B: "Nice to meet you John. No this is actually my first time. How about you?"

2. Building professional relationships:

Building professional relationships in networking is crucial for establishing long-term connections and potential collaborations. It involves cultivating trust effective communication and showing genuine interest in others' work and achievements. Engaging in meaningful conversations following up after events and offering assistance or resources when needed are key practices to build strong professional relationships.

Example:

Person A: "I heard you recently launched a new project. Could you tell me more about it?"

Person B: "Certainly! It's a software application that streamlines project management processes. I'd be happy to give you a demo if you're interested."

3. Overcoming cultural barriers in networking:

In a globalized world networking often involves interacting with individuals from diverse cultural backgrounds. Overcoming cultural barriers is essential to building effective connections. This includes understanding and respecting different communication styles social norms and values. It's important to be mindful of any potential language or cultural barriers and adapt communication accordingly such as using clear and simple language avoiding slang or non-verbal gestures that may be misunderstood.

Example:

Person A: "In my culture it's customary to exchange business cards. May I offer you mine?"

Person B: "Thank you for the offer. In my culture we usually prefer digital contact information. Can I connect with you on LinkedIn instead?"

By understanding and applying these principles individuals can enhance their networking skills establish meaningful connections and overcome potential barriers in the process.

Overall networking and socializing in a business setting are critical elements for professional success. By actively engaging with others professionals can expand their networks learn from industry experts collaborate on projects and build a strong personal brand. By fostering meaningful relationships and establishing trust individuals can open doors to new opportunities gain access to valuable resources and advance their careers.

III

Business English for Specific Situations

"Business English for Specific Situations" tailors language skills to precise corporate contexts. Unveil the power of impactful job applications and interviews, while also mastering the language of international business travel. Delve into cross-cultural communication, understanding its intricacies and avoiding potential conflicts. With ethical considerations and diplomatic solutions, this segment prepares you for a myriad of real-world scenarios.

Job Application and Interview Skills

Business ethics refers to the moral principles and values that guide the behavior and decision-making within a business setting. It encompasses concepts such as honesty integrity fairness and respect for others. Business ethics sets the standard for how businesses should operate ensuring that they act in ways that are both legally and morally acceptable.

Ethics in business involves making choices that are ethically responsible and justifiable even when faced with challenging situations. This includes treating employees customers suppliers and competitors with fairness and respect. It also involves maintaining transparency in business operations adhering to legal requirements and striving for social responsibility.

Business etiquette on the other hand refers to the set of rules and norms that govern professional behavior and interactions in a business environment. It focuses on respecting social conventions and demonstrating professionalism in all aspects of business conduct. Business etiquette encompasses various areas including communication dress code punctuality manners and networking.

Communication etiquette in business involves using proper language and tone in written and verbal communication. It also involves active listening providing timely responses and practicing courtesy and respect in all interactions.

Dress code etiquette dictates appropriate attire for different business settings ensuring that individuals present themselves professionally and adhere to the dress expectations of their industry or organization.

Punctuality is an essential aspect of business etiquette as it reflects professionalism and respect for others' time. Being punctual for meetings appointments and deadlines demonstrates reliability and accountability.

Manners and politeness are crucial in business etiquette involving showing respect and consideration towards others. This includes using proper greetings and introductions expressing gratitude and practicing good table manners during business meals or social events.

Networking etiquette is about building and maintaining professional relationships. It involves approaching people appropriately exchanging business cards following up after meetings or events and respecting others' boundaries.

Overall business ethics and etiquette are interconnected as ethical behavior often aligns with good business practices and respectful conduct towards others. Adhering to ethical standards and practicing proper business etiquette can help establish a positive reputation for a business and enhance relationships with stakeholders.

- Ethical considerations in business communication: This involves adhering to moral and ethical principles when engaging in communication within a business context. It includes ensuring honesty integrity transparency and respect for others. One example of ethical considerations in business communication is when a company communicates with its customers about a product or service. It should provide accurate information avoid false advertising and not mislead or deceive customers.

- Professional etiquette and behavior: This pertains to following proper norms and protocols in a professional setting. It involves maintaining professionalism good manners and respectfulness towards colleagues clients and stakeholders. One example of professional etiquette is using appropriate language and tone in emails or meetings with colleagues avoiding offensive or inappropriate comments and showing respect for diverse perspectives.

- Handling difficult situations diplomatically: This refers to managing challenging or potentially contentious situations in a tactful and considerate manner. It involves finding a balanced approach to resolve conflicts or address sensitive issues without causing unnecessary harm or damage. An example of handling difficult situations diplomatically is when a manager provides constructive feedback to an employee. They should use an empathetic and constructive approach to avoid demotivating the employee while addressing the issue at hand.

Vocabulary words and examples:

1. Integrity: Keeping one's word and acting in a trustworthy manner. For example a business leader who refuses to engage in any bribery or corruption demonstrates integrity.

2. Transparency: Being open and honest in communication sharing information freely and providing clear explanations. For instance a company that publishes its financial reports for public review exhibits transparency.

3. Respectfulness: Showing consideration and courtesy towards others. An example would be addressing colleagues by their preferred name and using appropriate language in professional conversations.

4. Tactful: Involving being diplomatic and sensitive when communicating or dealing with others. For instance offering suggestions for improvement without criticizing or embarrassing someone.

5. Constructive feedback: Providing feedback that focuses on improvement

and offers specific suggestions for growth. For example a manager giving feedback to an employee about their presentation skills and suggesting areas for improvement.

6. Empathetic: Understanding and sharing the feelings of others. An example would be showing empathy towards an employee who is going through a difficult personal situation and being understanding and supportive.

Using these vocabulary words in communication and behavior can enhance professional etiquette and ethical considerations.

Business Travel and Tourism

English job application and interview skills are essential for anyone seeking employment in an English-speaking country or company. These skills involve effectively communicating your qualifications experiences and skills in written and spoken English to employers.

In terms of job applications mastering English skills is crucial for writing a compelling resume and cover letter. In the resume you need to showcase your educational background work experience and skills in a clear and concise manner. You should use correct grammar punctuation and vocabulary to create a professional impression. For example instead of saying "I did" or "I have done use more formal language such as "I achieved" or "I have accomplished."

In the cover letter you need to explain why you are interested in the position and how your qualifications align with the job requirements. You should demonstrate your written communication skills by structuring your sentences well and expressing your ideas coherently. Additionally you should showcase your knowledge of the company and industry to show your enthusiasm and dedication. For instance instead of saying "I want to work for your company you could say "I am drawn to your company's innovative approach and extensive impact in the technology industry."

During the interview process your English skills will be tested in both verbal and non-verbal communication. Here are a few key points to remember:

1. Listen attentively: Pay close attention to the interviewer's questions and listen carefully before providing your response. Active listening demonstrates your ability to understand and follow instructions.

2. Speak clearly and confidently: Enunciate your words clearly and speak at a moderate pace. Avoid using excessive jargon or technical terms that the interviewer may not be familiar with. Confidence in your speech is important to show that you believe in your own abilities.

3. Provide examples: Support your responses with concrete examples from your personal or professional experience. Be specific and highlight your achievements and problem-solving skills. For example instead of saying "I am good at problem-solving you could say "In my previous role I implemented a new strategy that saved the company 20% in operational costs."

4. Ask questions: At the end of the interview the interviewer may ask if you have any questions. This is an opportunity for you to demonstrate your interest and curiosity in the company. Prepare a few thoughtful questions in advance based on your research of the company and the role.

Overall mastering English job application and interview skills requires practice and refinement. Take advantage of resources such as online courses practice interviews and feedback from native English speakers to improve your skills. With strong English communication abilities you will increase your chances of success in the competitive job market.

Writing a strong cover letter and resume

Writing a strong cover letter and resume is essential when it comes to applying for a job. They are often the first impression a potential employer has of you so it is crucial to make them stand out. Below are some tips and examples on how to create a powerful cover letter and resume.

1. Research: Before you start writing research the company and the job requirements. This will help you tailor your cover letter and resume to the specific position and show your genuine interest in the company.

Example: If you are applying for a marketing role at a tech startup highlight any past experience or skills that are relevant to this industry. Mention any successful marketing campaigns you have worked on or specific skills related to digital marketing.

2. Strong opening: Begin your cover letter with a strong opening statement that grabs the reader's attention. This should briefly summarize your skills experiences and why you are interested in the position.

Example: "As a creative and results-driven marketing professional with a passion for the tech industry I am excited to apply for the marketing role at ABC Tech. With my expertise in digital marketing and a proven track record of driving successful campaigns I am confident that I can contribute to the growth and success of your company."

3. Highlight achievements and skills: Use your resume to showcase your achievements skills and experiences that are relevant to the job you are applying for. Be specific and provide concrete examples of how you have contributed to previous roles or projects.

Example: Instead of simply stating "Managed social media accounts you could say "Managed social media accounts for a company increasing engagement by 25% and driving a 30% increase in website traffic."

4. Be concise: Keep your cover letter and resume concise and to the point. Avoid lengthy paragraphs and make sure to use bullet points to highlight key

information.

Example: Instead of writing a paragraph discussing your past job responsibilities break it down into bullet points to make it easier to read and scan.

5. Grammar and format: Pay attention to grammar spelling and formatting. Make sure your cover letter and resume are error-free and consistent in terms of formatting font and spacing.

Example: Use professional language and avoid slang or informal expressions. Proofread your documents multiple times or ask someone else to review them for you to catch any errors or inconsistencies.

Overall a strong cover letter and resume will showcase your skills experiences and enthusiasm for the position you are applying for. By tailoring them to the specific job requirements providing clear examples and paying attention to detail you can increase your chances of standing out among other applicants and landing the job.

Navigating job interviews in English

When it comes to navigating job interviews in English and impressing potential employers with your language skills there are several key aspects to consider. These include preparing beforehand showcasing your language abilities during the interview and emphasizing the benefits of your language skills to the employer.

1. Preparing beforehand:
Before the interview it's essential to research the company and position you're applying for thoroughly. Take note of any industry-related terminology or common interview questions that may arise. This preparation will help you

feel more confident and better prepared to showcase your language skills.

2. Showcasing language abilities during the interview:

During the interview it's crucial to actively demonstrate your language skills to the best of your ability. Here are a few ways you can do that:

- Speak clearly and confidently: Pay attention to your pronunciation intonation and fluency. Practice speaking in English beforehand to build your confidence and ensure clear communication.

- Use appropriate vocabulary and grammar: Employers will be impressed if you can showcase a wide range of vocabulary and use proper grammar structures. This includes using industry-specific terminology when applicable.

- Active listening and responding: Demonstrate your ability to understand and respond to questions effectively. Take your time to comprehend the question and provide thoughtful and articulate answers.

- Non-verbal communication: Pay attention to your body language such as maintaining eye contact using appropriate gestures and displaying good posture. Non-verbal cues are equally important in conveying your language skills and professionalism.

3. Emphasizing the benefits of your language skills:

In addition to showcasing your language abilities it's important to highlight the specific benefits your language skills can bring to the employer. This includes:

- Communication with clients or customers: Emphasize your ability to communicate effectively with international clients or customers who may speak English as their first language. Highlight your cross-cultural understanding and language proficiency as an asset in building strong relationships.

- Collaboration and teamwork: Discuss how your language skills can facilitate effective communication and collaboration with diverse teams. Highlight how you can bridge language barriers and facilitate better understanding among team members.

- Representation and internationalization: If the company has global aspirations or deals with international markets emphasize how your language skills can contribute to their expansion plans and represent the company effectively in global settings.

Example:

During an interview for a marketing position you can showcase your language skills in the following ways:

- Speaking clearly and confidently in English using marketing-related vocabulary to demonstrate your understanding of the industry.
- Discussing your experience in collaborating with international teams and how your language skills have helped you bridge communication gaps and build successful campaigns.
- Highlighting your ability to communicate with clients or customers from diverse cultural backgrounds showcasing your cross-cultural understanding and adaptability.

Overall by preparing beforehand showcasing your language abilities during the interview and emphasizing the benefits of your language skills to the employer you can navigate job interviews in English confidently and leave a positive impression on potential employers.

Vocabulary words which used for job interview

1. Leadership: "I have demonstrated strong leadership skills in my previous role where I successfully led a team of 10 individuals."
2. Teamwork: "I believe that effective teamwork is crucial in achieving company goals and I have a proven track record of collaborating with colleagues

to drive successful projects."

3. Communication: "I am confident in my ability to effectively communicate with both internal and external stakeholders which has allowed me to build strong relationships and contribute to successful outcomes."

4. Adaptability: "In a fast-paced industry I have shown my ability to quickly adapt to new processes and technologies allowing me to consistently meet changing customer demands."

5. Problem-solving: "When faced with a challenge I take a proactive approach to problem-solving considering different perspectives and exploring innovative solutions."

6. Time management: "Through effective time management skills I have consistently met tight deadlines and successfully prioritized tasks to ensure productivity and efficiency."

7. Organization: "I have a strong attention to detail and have implemented organizational systems in my previous roles which have resulted in improved productivity and streamlined processes."

8. Decision-making: "I am confident in my ability to make informed decisions by analyzing available data and considering potential risks and benefits."

9. Critical thinking: "I have a strong ability to think critically and analyze complex situations which has allowed me to make well-informed decisions under pressure."

10. Goal-oriented: "I am highly motivated and set clear goals for myself which helps me stay focused and driven to achieve results."

11. Creativity: "I approach problem-solving and tasks with a creative mindset often thinking outside the box to generate innovative ideas and find unique solutions."

12. Flexibility: "I am adaptable to changing circumstances and can quickly adjust my plans and strategies when necessary."

13. Initiative: "I am proactive in identifying opportunities for improvement and taking action without waiting for instructions which has resulted in increased efficiency and positive outcomes."

14. Analytical: "I possess strong analytical skills and can effectively analyze

data to identify trends and make informed decisions."

15. Client focus: "I believe in understanding the needs of the client and strive to provide exceptional service that exceeds their expectations."

16. Business acumen: "I have a strong understanding of the business industry and can make strategic decisions that align with the company's objectives."

17. Networking: "I actively engage in networking opportunities to build relationships and expand professional connections which has resulted in new business opportunities and partnerships."

18. Conflict resolution: "I have experience in effectively resolving conflicts and maintaining positive working relationships through open communication and finding mutually beneficial solutions."

19. Presentation skills: "I am confident in my ability to deliver engaging and impactful presentations utilizing visual aids and effective communication techniques to convey complex information."

20. Negotiation: "I possess strong negotiation skills and have successfully reached mutually beneficial agreements in various professional settings."

21. Problem analysis: "I am skilled in analyzing complex problems by breaking them down into manageable components which allows me to identify root causes and implement effective solutions."

22. Initiative-taking: "I am proactive in identifying opportunities for improvement and taking action without waiting for instructions which has resulted in increased efficiency and positive outcomes."

23. Resilience: "I am able to bounce back from setbacks and maintain a positive mindset which allows me to persevere and overcome challenges."

24. Detail-oriented: "I have a keen eye for detail and can ensure accuracy in tasks and projects minimizing errors and maximizing overall quality."

25. Multitasking: "I am adept at handling multiple tasks simultaneously and can effectively prioritize and manage my workload to meet deadlines."

26. Emotional intelligence: "I possess strong emotional intelligence and can effectively understand and manage my own emotions as well as empathize with others leading to strong interpersonal relationships."

27. Technical expertise: "I have advanced technical expertise in my field

allowing me to confidently utilize specialized software or equipment to achieve exceptional results."

28. Conflict management: "I have experience in effectively managing conflicts by actively listening seeking common ground and facilitating open and productive discussions."

29. Team building: "I have a proven ability to build and foster strong teams by creating a positive work environment encouraging collaboration and recognizing individual contributions."

30. Continuous learning: "I am committed to continuous learning and development consistently seeking new knowledge and skills to stay up-to-date in the rapidly evolving business landscape."

31. Data analysis: "I am experienced in analyzing large sets of complex data using various software and tools to draw insights and make data-driven decisions."

32. Decision-making: "I approach decision-making with a systematic and logical approach considering all relevant factors and potential impacts before reaching a conclusion."

33. Innovation: "I actively seek opportunities for innovation and improvement challenging the status quo and proposing creative ideas that drive positive change."

34. Relationship building: "I have a natural ability to build rapport and establish strong relationships with colleagues clients and stakeholders helping to foster trust and collaboration."

35. Strategic thinking: "I possess a strategic mindset and can think critically about long-term goals and objectives aligning my actions with the overall direction of the organization."

36. Judgment: "I have strong judgment skills and can make informed decisions by evaluating available information and considering potential risks and benefits."

37. Resourcefulness: "I am highly resourceful and can find creative solutions to problems even with limited resources or challenging circumstances."

38. Interpersonal skills: "I have excellent interpersonal skills and can effectively communicate and relate to individuals at all levels of an organization."

39. Self-motivation: "I am internally driven and have a strong sense of self-motivation which allows me to stay focused and productive even in challenging situations."

40. Emotional resilience: "I am able to remain calm and composed in high-pressure situations and I can effectively manage stress and emotions to maintain a consistent level of performance."

41. Growth mindset: "I have a growth mindset believing that skills and abilities can be developed through persistence and effort allowing me to continuously learn and improve."

42. Cultural awareness: "I possess cultural awareness and sensitivity understanding and respecting differences and effectively engaging with individuals from diverse backgrounds."

43. Customer service: "I have a strong customer service orientation and can effectively anticipate and meet customer needs resulting in high customer satisfaction and repeat business."

44. Salesmanship: "I have a natural ability to persuade and influence others and I can effectively communicate the value of a product or service to potential customers."

45. Budgeting: "I am adept at budgeting and financial planning ensuring that resources are allocated effectively and financial goals are met."

46. Conflict resolution: "I have experience in effectively resolving conflicts and maintaining positive working relationships through open communication and finding mutually beneficial solutions."

47. Delegation: "I can delegate tasks effectively matching skills and strengths to optimize team productivity and ensure successful outcomes."

48. Accountability: "I take ownership of my actions and accept responsibility for my performance holding myself to high standards of professionalism and integrity."

49. Networking: "I actively engage in networking opportunities to build relationships and expand professional connections which has resulted in new business opportunities and partnerships."

50. Time management: "Through effective time management skills I have consistently met tight deadlines and successfully prioritized tasks to ensure

productivity and efficiency."

Cross-Cultural Communication in Business

Business travel and tourism refers to individuals usually professionals who travel for the purpose of conducting business activities or attending business-related events. It involves the combination of traveling to a different location for work-related purposes and engaging in tourism activities during leisure time.

Business travel has become an integral part of the global economy as companies expand their operations beyond their local markets. This type of travel encompasses a wide range of activities including attending conferences meetings trade shows client visits training programs and negotiations with business partners. It allows companies to establish and maintain business relationships explore new markets and expand their operations.

The tourism aspect of business travel refers to the leisure activities that individuals engage in during their free time while on a business trip. This could include visiting tourist attractions exploring local culture trying local cuisine shopping or participating in recreational activities. This aspect of business travel offers an opportunity for professionals to experience new destinations and gain a broader perspective on different cultures and societies.

The business travel and tourism industry encompasses a variety of sectors including transportation accommodation food and beverage entertainment and travel services. Airlines hotels travel agencies and car rental companies are some of the key players in this industry. These sectors cater to the specific needs and requirements of business travelers by offering services such as convenient flight schedules comfortable accommodations conference facilities and efficient transportation options.

Business travel and tourism contribute significantly to the global economy. It generates revenue for various sectors and creates employment opportunities. According to the World Travel and Tourism Council (WTTC business travel and tourism accounted for approximately 21% of global travel and tourism expenditure in 2019.

However the COVID-19 pandemic has had a profound impact on business travel and tourism. Travel restrictions lockdowns and the shift towards remote work have significantly reduced the demand for business travel. Companies have adopted virtual meetings and online conferences as an alternative to in-person events. The industry is adapting to these challenges by implementing health and safety measures re-evaluating travel policies and exploring new opportunities such as hybrid events that combine virtual and in-person experiences.

In conclusion business travel and tourism play a vital role in the global economy by facilitating meetings fostering business relationships and providing leisure opportunities for professionals. While the industry faces challenges due to the pandemic it continues to adapt and innovate to meet the changing needs and expectations of business travelers.

Common phrases for travel and accommodation

1. "Do you have any rooms available for tonight?"
2. "How much is the room per night?"
3. "Can I have a room with a view?"

4. "Is breakfast included in the price?"

5. "What time is check-in/check-out?"

6. "Could you please recommend some nearby restaurants?"

7. "Is there a shuttle service to the airport/train station?"

8. "Are there any extra charges for amenities like Wi-Fi or parking?"

9. "Could you please provide me with a map of the local area?"

10. "Do you have a safe deposit box available?"

11. "Are there any laundry facilities or services?"

12. "Is there a gym or fitness center in the hotel?"

13. "Is it possible to request a wake-up call?"

14. "Could I have an extra pillow/blanket/towel?"

15. "Is there an elevator in the building?"

16. "Is smoking allowed in the room?"

17. "Is there a cancellation policy?"

18. "Are pets allowed in the hotel?"

19. "Can I pay with a credit card?"

20. "Is there a nearby pharmacy/supermarket/bank?"

21. "Do you have a concierge service available?"

22. "What are the transportation options to the city center?"

23. "Is there a tourist information center nearby?"

24. "Can I exchange currency at the hotel?"

25. "Are there any cultural events or attractions happening during my stay?"

26. "Could you please recommend some sightseeing spots in the area?"

27. "Do you offer any guided tours?"

28. "Is there a car rental service available?"

29. "What are the popular local dishes that I must try?"

30. "Are there any specific dress codes or customs to be aware of in this area?"

31. "Can you please book a table for dinner at a local restaurant?"

32. "Are there any festivals or events happening during my stay?"

33. "What is the best way to get to the airport/train station?"

34. "Is there a late-night dining option available in the hotel?"

35. "Are there any discounts or promotions available for longer stays?"

36. "Can I store my luggage at the hotel after check-out?"
37. "Is there a swimming pool in the hotel?"
38. "Do you have any allergy-friendly options in the restaurant?"
39. "Could you please help me arrange transportation for a day trip?"
40. "Is there a spa or wellness center in the hotel?"
41. "Can I request a quiet room away from the street?"
42. "What is the voltage in the country and do I need a power adapter?"
43. "Do you provide airport/train station transfers?"
44. "Is there any nearby public transportation?"
45. "Can I have a non-smoking room please?"
46. "Are there any vegetarian/vegan options in the restaurant?"
47. "Do you offer room service?"
48. "Could you please arrange a taxi for me?"
49. "Is there a luggage storage service available?"
50. "Are there any cultural or historical sites within walking distance?"

Communicating effectively with hotels and restaurants

When it comes to communication with hotels and restaurants there are several key factors to keep in mind in order to effectively communicate your needs and resolve any issues that may arise.

Firstly it's important to be clear and concise in your communication. Whether you are making a reservation requesting a specific room or table or inquiring about amenities or services be specific about what you need or expect. Clearly state your preferences such as dietary restrictions or room preferences to ensure that the hotel or restaurant can accommodate your needs.

Additionally it's essential to use appropriate and polite language when communicating with hotel and restaurant staff. Politeness and respect go a long way in establishing positive relationships and ensuring that your requests are taken seriously. Remember to use "please" and "thank you" when making requests or expressing gratitude.

If you encounter any problems or have concerns during your stay or meal it's important to address them promptly and calmly. Rather than getting angry or confrontational approach the staff with a polite and understanding demeanor. Clearly explain the issue or concern and work together with them to find a solution. This collaborative approach is more likely to result in a satisfactory resolution.

When traveling for business it's also important to communicate your needs and requirements in advance. This includes informing the hotel or restaurant about any specific requests or arrangements required for meetings or events. Providing a detailed itinerary of your schedule and requirements can help ensure that everything is prepared accordingly.

In addition it's wise to have a point of contact within the hotel or restaurant for any last-minute changes or emergencies. This can be a designated staff member or the hotel's front desk. Establishing this communication channel can make it easier to handle unexpected situations and make necessary adjustments.

Lastly it's crucial to keep records of all your communication. This includes confirmation emails receipts and any correspondence related to your stay or meal arrangements. These documents can be useful for reference and can help resolve any disputes or misunderstandings that may occur later on.

Overall effective communication with hotels and restaurants involves clear and polite communication addressing issues promptly and maintaining good records. By following these guidelines you can ensure a smooth and enjoyable experience during your travels for business.

Business Ethics and Etiquette

Cross-cultural communication in business refers to the communication and interaction between individuals or groups from different cultures in a business setting. It involves understanding and adapting to the cultural differences and nuances to ensure effective communication collaboration and business success.

One example of cross-cultural communication in business is negotiating contracts. In some cultures negotiations are expected to be direct assertive and focused on bottom-line results. However in other cultures negotiations are more indirect building relationships and reaching consensus before reaching a decision. For instance in Japan negotiations may involve several meetings and discussions before a final agreement is reached. It is important for business professionals to understand and respect these cultural preferences to avoid misunderstandings and build successful partnerships.

Another example is team meetings. In a multicultural team different cultures may have different norms regarding hierarchy decision-making processes and communication styles. For instance in some cultures team members may not openly express disagreement or ask questions to avoid confrontation or appearing disrespectful. In contrast others may encourage open and lively discussions. Effective cross-cultural communication in team meetings involves creating a safe and inclusive environment where all team members feel comfortable expressing their ideas and concerns. It also requires using clear and concise language avoiding jargon or idioms that may not be understood by all and actively listening to and valuing different perspectives.

Additionally cross-cultural communication is vital in marketing and advertising. Different cultures have distinct preferences values and communication styles. What may be effective and appealing in one culture can be considered offensive or irrelevant in another. For example colors symbols and imagery can have different meanings across cultures. Therefore careful consideration and adaptation of marketing strategies are necessary to ensure effective communication and resonate with the target audience. Global brands often modify their advertising campaigns to suit local cultural sensitivities and preferences.

Understanding cultural differences in communication: This topic refers to the awareness and knowledge of how cultural backgrounds can influence the way people communicate. It involves recognizing that different cultures have unique communication styles norms and expectations. For instance in some cultures direct and assertive communication is favored while in others indirect and subtle communication is valued.

Example: In Japan there is a cultural norm of high context communication which means that much is conveyed through nonverbal cues and indirect gestures. This can include using silence as a way to show respect or agreement. Understanding this cultural difference is important for effective communication with Japanese colleagues or clients as explicitly stating disagreement or criticism can be seen as disrespectful.

Adapting to different business norms and practices: This topic relates to the ability to adjust and conform to the specific customs behaviors and practices within different business environments. Each culture has its own conventions regarding business etiquette negotiations decision-making processes and professional relationships.

Example: In China building a personal relationship or Guanxi is highly valued in business. This means that before engaging in any substantial business discussion it is common to spend time getting to know each other on a personal level such as through meals or social activities. Adapting to this practice is vital for establishing trust and successful business relationships in Chinese contexts.

Avoiding cultural misunderstandings and conflicts: This topic encompasses the skills and strategies needed to prevent misunderstandings and conflicts that may arise from cultural differences. It involves being sensitive and respectful towards diverse cultural perspectives as well as being open-minded and willing to bridge gaps in understanding.

Example: In the United States direct and open communication is often embraced even in a confrontational manner. However in some collectivist cultures such as many Asian cultures open confrontation can be seen as disrespectful and damaging to relationships. Being aware of this difference and finding alternative ways to address conflicts can help avoid misunderstandings and foster positive relationships in cross-cultural settings.

In summary understanding cultural differences in communication involves recognizing the impact of cultural backgrounds on communication styles adapting to different business norms and practices and preventing cultural misunderstandings and conflicts through sensitivity and open-mindedness.

Phrases used in business English

Here are some important examples of phrases used in business English:

1. "Please find attached the sales report for the month of October."

2. "I am writing to inquire about your product availability and pricing."

3. "Thank you for considering our proposal. We look forward to hearing your feedback."

4. "I would like to schedule a meeting to discuss the project further. Can we meet on Tuesday at 9 am?"

5. "Could you please provide me with a quote for the services requested?"

6. "I apologize for the inconvenience caused. We are investigating the issue and will provide a resolution as soon as possible."

7. "Our company is interested in forming a partnership with your organization. Can we arrange a meeting to discuss the details?"

8. "Please confirm receipt of this email."

9. "We appreciate your prompt response to our inquiry."

10. "I have attached the contract for your review and signature."

11. "Thank you for your order. We will process it and provide you with a tracking number shortly."

12. "Please let me know if you require any further information or assistance."

13. "We are pleased to inform you that your application has been accepted. Congratulations!"

14. "Could you please provide me with an update on the status of the project?"

15. "I apologize for the delay in responding. I was out of the office attending a conference."

100 Phrases used in business English:

1. Can you please send me the updated sales report?
2. We need to have a conference call to discuss the new marketing strategy.
3. I will schedule a meeting with the client next week.
4. Let's set up a performance review for all employees.
5. Please review the terms and conditions before signing the contract.
6. We apologize for the inconvenience and are working to resolve the issue.
7. Our company offers a wide range of products and services.
8. Could you provide me with an estimate for the project?
9. We are experiencing a high demand for our latest product.
10. We appreciate your timely response to our request.
11. The quarterly financial report indicates a positive growth trend.
12. We need to improve our customer service to enhance satisfaction levels.
13. The marketing department is planning a new advertising campaign.
14. Our team has successfully completed the project ahead of schedule.
15. We will need to negotiate the terms of the partnership agreement.
16. We value your feedback and suggestions for improvement.
17. The sales team surpassed their monthly target.

18. The CEO will deliver a speech at the annual shareholders' meeting.

19. We need to streamline our production process to reduce costs.

20. The company is seeking investors for our upcoming expansion plans.

21. Our team has identified new potential clients in the market.

22. The project requires collaboration between different departments.

23. We need to conduct market research to identify new opportunities.

24. The training program will enhance employees' skills and knowledge.

25. We would like to propose a new pricing strategy for our products.

26. The IT department is responsible for managing our network infrastructure.

27. We aim to achieve a sustainable growth strategy for the company.

28. Our company values diversity and promotes an inclusive work environment.

29. The HR department is responsible for recruiting and selecting new staff.

30. Our team will be attending the industry conference next month.

31. We need to analyze the competition to stay ahead in the market.

32. The new website design will improve the user experience.

33. The finance department will prepare the budget for the upcoming year.

34. We need to invest in new equipment to increase productivity.

35. Our company offers excellent after-sales support for our customers.

36. We need to enhance our online presence through social media marketing.

37. The legal team is reviewing the contract for any potential risks.

38. The company's mission is to provide innovative solutions to our clients.

39. We encourage employees to participate in professional development programs.

40. Our company adheres to strict quality control standards.

41. The marketing campaign resulted in a significant increase in sales.

42. The project manager will oversee the implementation of the new system.

43. We need to conduct a SWOT analysis to assess our strengths and weaknesses.

44. We will need to file for a patent to protect our invention.

45. The customer service team handles all customer inquiries and complaints.

46. We need to adapt to the changing market trends to remain competitive.

47. The company has a clear vision and sets ambitious goals.

48. We need to improve our supply chain to ensure timely deliveries.

49. The executive team is working on a strategic plan for the future.

50. Our company is committed to sustainable and ethical business practices.

51. We need to conduct a feasibility study before launching the new product.

52. The project requires a detailed cost estimation to secure funding.

53. We will need to conduct staff training on the new software.

54. Our company has achieved ISO certification for quality management.

55. We need to review and update our employee handbook.

56. We will need to implement a performance appraisal system.

57. The marketing team is preparing a targeted advertising campaign.

58. We need to improve our customer retention strategies.

59. The finance team will prepare financial forecasts for the next fiscal year.

60. Our company is expanding into new international markets.

61. We will need to analyze the market trends to identify growth opportunities.

62. We need to establish key performance indicators for each department.

63. The project requires a strong collaboration between internal and external stakeholders.

64. We will need to negotiate the terms of the supplier contract.

65. Our company is committed to corporate social responsibility initiatives.

66. We need to diversify our product portfolio to minimize risk.

67. The sales team will attend a training workshop on closing deals.

68. We need to re brand our company to target a younger demographic.

69. The IT department is responsible for data security and privacy.

70. We aim to build long-term relationships with our clients.

71. We need to analyze the market to identify potential threats.

72. The marketing team will create a promotional campaign for the new product.

73. We will need to secure additional funding for the expansion project.

74. Our company offers competitive salary packages to attract top talent.

75. We need to assess the risks associated with the project.

76. The human resources team is responsible for employee benefits and payroll.

77. We need to create a project timeline to ensure timely completion.

78. The operational team will streamline processes to increase efficiency.

79. We will need to conduct a customer satisfaction survey.

80. Our company values teamwork and fosters a collaborative culture.

81. We need to analyze the return on investment for the marketing campaign.

82. The project requires a comprehensive market analysis report.

83. We will need to develop a contingency plan for any potential disruptions.

84. The research and development team will innovate new product features.

85. We need to improve our inventory management to minimize stock-outs.

86. Our company strives for continuous improvement in all areas.

87. We will need to implement a customer relationship management system.

88. The project requires adherence to strict quality control standards.

89. We need to create a strong brand identity for our company.

90. The marketing team will conduct focus groups to gather consumer insights.

91. We will need to evaluate the financial viability of potential investments.

92. Our company promotes a culture of open communication and transparency.

93. We need to develop a strong marketing strategy to penetrate new markets.

94. The project manager will assign tasks to team members.

95. We will need to present the business plan to potential investors.

96. Our company is committed to reducing our carbon footprint.

97. We need to address any customer complaints in a timely manner.

98. The IT team will upgrade our systems to improve performance.

99. We will need to allocate resources effectively to complete the project.

100. Our company aims to be a leader in the industry through innovation.

Extra 50 phrases for daily office life:

1. Good morning, everyone!
2. How was your weekend?
3. Let's get started, shall we?
4. I have a quick question.
5. Can you help me with this?
6. Just a heads up...
7. I'll be in a meeting until noon.
8. Could you please send me that file?
9. It's on my to-do list.
10. I'll take care of that right away.
11. Could you give me a hand?
12. Thanks for your input.
13. The deadline is approaching.
14. Let's touch base later.
15. We need to brainstorm some ideas.
16. I'll send out the agenda.
17. What's the status on this project?
18. Any updates on the client's response?
19. Can we schedule a conference call?
20. I'll book a meeting room.
21. Can you run that by me again?
22. Let's run it by the team.
23. I'm on it!
24. I'll make the necessary arrangements.
25. We should circle back on this.
26. Do you have a minute?
27. Let's work out the details.
28. Don't forget to RSVP for the event.
29. I appreciate your effort.
30. This report needs some revisions.
31. I'll prepare the presentation slides.
32. It's a work in progress.
33. Could you provide some feedback?

34. Let's iron out the logistics.

35. The printer is out of paper again.

36. Can you fill me in on the details?

37. It's time for the team meeting.

38. We're making great progress.

39. I'm attending a workshop today.

40. Let's schedule a one-on-one.

41. The software update is complete.

42. We're experiencing technical difficulties.

43. Please keep me in the loop.

44. I'll send out a reminder email.

45. I'll take care of the billing.

46. We're facing a tight deadline.

47. I have a conflicting appointment.

48. Could you pass me the stapler?

49. Let's plan a team-building activity.

50. I'm looking forward to the company retreat.

www.ingramcontent.com/pod-product-compliance
Lightning Source LLC
Chambersburg PA
CBHW062342290526
45794CB00005B/2081